First published in India in 2018 by HarperCollins *Children's* Books
An imprint of HarperCollins *Publishers*
A-75, Sector 57, Noida, Uttar Pradesh 201301, India
www.harpercollins.co.in

2 4 6 8 10 9 7 5 3 1

P-ISBN: 978-93-5277-744-0

Printed and bound at
Nutech Print Services - India

THE GOOD INDIAN CHILD'S GUIDE TO EATING MANGOES!

Natasha Sharma

Illustrated by
Shreya Sen

HarperCollins*Children's Books*

That's the author, Natasha Sharma? Nah! She doesn't look like an author.

What do you mean she doesn't look like an author? She's written 18 books for children!

So what? Where's the serious face? Where are the specs perched on her nose? Is that mango on her cheeks?

Her books have won awards! Her poems are in coursebooks for children. Did I mention 18 books?

That may be, but which proper author writes a book on mangoes and ways to eat them? What's the moral of this story?

Moral? Moral! EAT MORE MANGOES AND READ MORE BOOKS! There's your moral! Psst: Hop across to www.natashasharma.in to find out more about the very real and proper author, Natasha.

Shreya Sen? That's the illustrator? Well, at least she has spectacles.

What's the obsession with spectacles? Shreya's a fancy one — studied Animation Film Design at NID, Ahmedabad. She interned at a children's publication house and decided that she wanted to be a children's book illustrator for the rest of her life.

So, she's illustrated many books, has she?

Loads of them! And she drew on walls as a kid. That counts for something.

Ha! I can draw on a wall.

Not as well as she can. She can also make chai and drink it. And she loves comics.

What?

And she can procrastinate and analyse narratives. Though not at the same time because then she wouldn't be procrastinating.

What?

Told you she's fancy. Check out https://sagoli-sagoli.blogspot.in/ to know more about her fancy work. Or you can write to her at shreyasensagoli@gmail.com

An
author's full disclosure:
Many mangoes have been hurt in
the making of this book. The author has
been a mango-eating fiend from her days of
being in a diaper and continues to munch them
to this day. The writing of this book led to
mango cravings more than ever before and
many trips to the fridge to cut up a mango.
Her dear friend, Anushka Ravishankar, who
helped with the first cut, claims that the
text leads to mango cravings. The
editor ordered a round of mango
milkshake for the office on
receiving the manuscript,
while the illustrator
went missing in
action for days.

This is a good Indian child.

She loves mangoes.

This is a good Indian child.

He loves mangoes.

Step 1
Get a mango.

To do this, you must know how to pick the best one.

A mango is at its best when it is firm, ripe and cold.

Or when it is firm,

ripe and just off a tree.

Or when it is firm, ripe and has been scooped out of the water tub where it lay soaking.

Or when it is softer than it should be but can be turned into a mango milkshake.

Or even when it has just been broken off a tree and is still raw and freeze-your-face so

Step 2
Know your
mango.

To know your friend, you must talk to your friend.

To know your mango, you do not need to talk to your mango.

You do not need to tell it a joke like this one:

"Man-going to eat you."

You just need to identify it. What type of a mango is it?

IS IT AN ALPHONSO, THE KING OF MANGOES?

Is it a **SMOOTH** and delicious, great-for-a-milkshake safeda?

Is it a get-stuck-in-your-teeth-full-of-threads green langda?

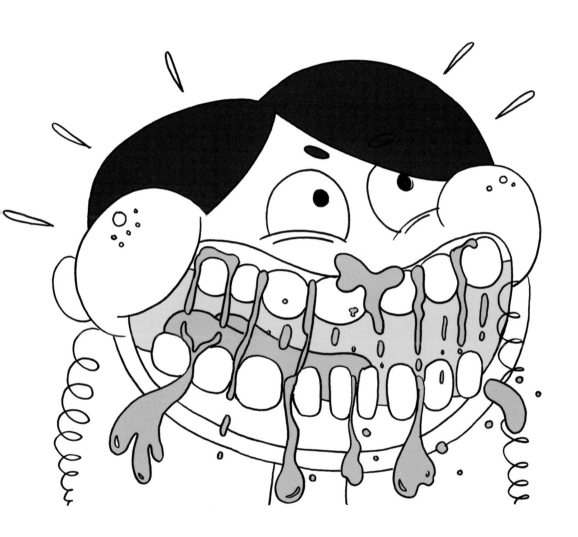

Is it a tiny tapka?

AN EQUAL-TO-TWO-MANGOES, GIGANTIC BANGANAPALLI OR RAJAPURI?

Perhaps the sweet-like-sugar chausa?

A parrot-beaked totapuri?

Step 3

Answer these

important questions.

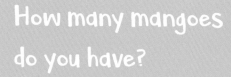

If there is only one mango amongst a bunch of you, do you plan to be a good Indian child and share it or ...

do you plan to be a good Indian child and ...

... grab it and run?

Is this instead a secret mango-eating mission?

Are you hiding and eating more mangoes than you should? This will determine the need for speed.

Do you have equipment like

a knife,

a spoon

and a plate

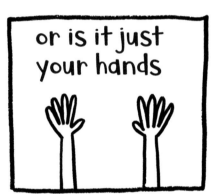

or is it just your hands

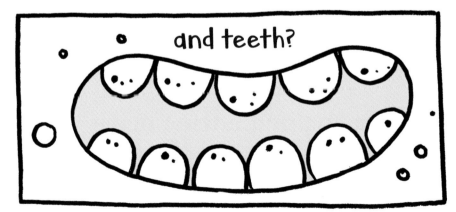

and teeth?

Save your fingers! Ask an adult for help!

Step 4
Know yourself.

TO ENJOY YOUR MANGO, YOU MUST KNOW YOURSELF.

Place the mango to one side and pay close attention.

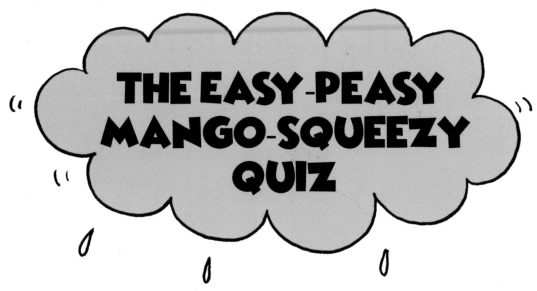

THE EASY-PEASY MANGO-SQUEEZY QUIZ

This easy quiz will help you decide the mango-eating way best suited to your personality.

I am:
(a) a neat and clean, napkin-in-lap sort of person.

(b) a messy, fought-a-war-with-my-napkin-now-on-the-floor sort.

(a) a 'Thank you', 'You're welcome', 'Good evening', 'I look forward to it' sort of person.

(b) a 'Huh? Who are you?', 'Leave me alone', 'Whatever!' kind.

(a) a nose-buried-in-a-book-as-I-wait, lost-track-of-time sort of person.

(b) a 'How much longer? Is it done yet? Are we there yet?' kind.

If you have two or more 'a's, try 'How to Eat a Mango' options 2, 3 or 7 that follow.

If you have two or more 'b's, try 'How to Eat a Mango' options 1, 5 or 6 that follow.

Option 8 can go either way.

Option 4 is not recommended for anyone without proper training.

Step 5
How to eat a mango in a few easy steps.

In case you missed that, here is where we finally get to the ways to eat a mango. This is a big deal. An important moment in the course of this book. We ask you to pause for a second and think of a juicy mango in your mouth.

You may now proceed to drool.

Read on for eight popular ways to eat a mango.

1) The Mango Massage Method
Also known as The Jungle Way

Give your mango a good massage by squishing it between your thumb and fingers. Make sure you loosen any tight lumps. It must feel squelchy.

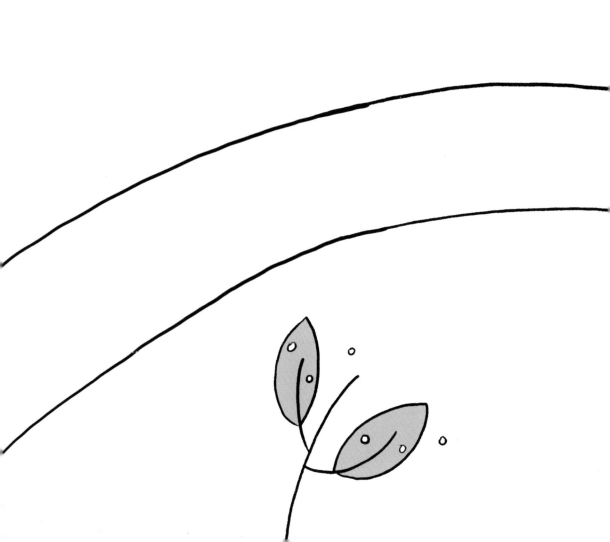

Nip off a tiny bit of skin from the top, either with your teeth ...

or with a knife.

Save your fingers! Ask an adult for help!

Place your mouth on the opening, squeeze the mango and **SUCK**.

...SRRROO

...OO...

OOO...OOO

O...O...

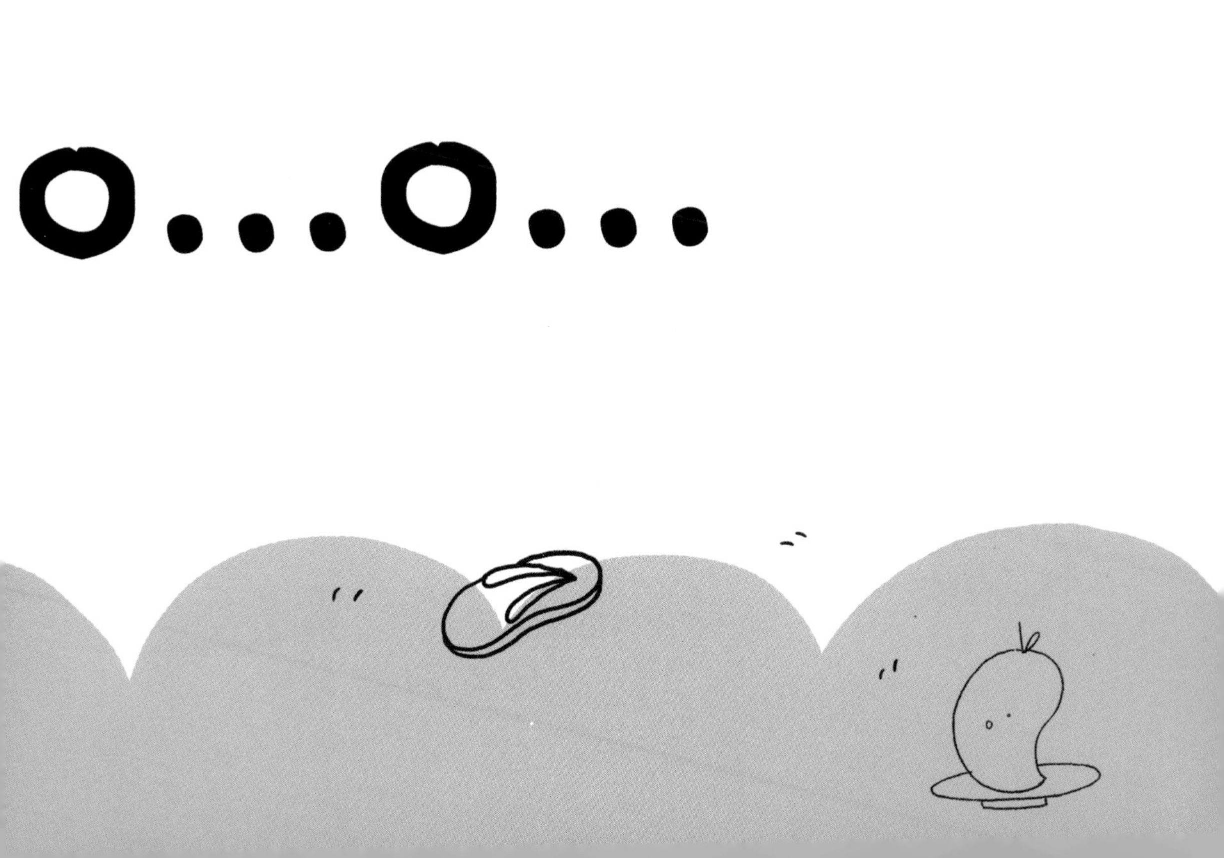

When the
SROOOOP
is getting
stuck,
squeeze out the
seed onto a plate.

2) The Big Scoop
Also known as The Big Boat

Cut two large pieces off either side of the seed.

CUT

 Save your fingers! Ask an adult for help!

You should now have two
BOAT-SHAPED CHUNKS
and one seed.

Spoon out big chunks from the mango boats.

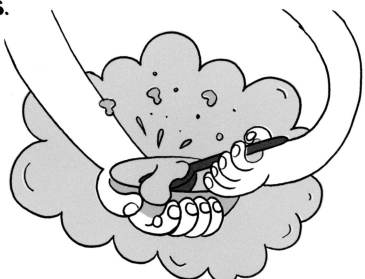

Transfer to your mouth for satisfying BIG scoops of mango.

Peel the skin from around the seed and scrape all remaining bits of the mango off the seed using your teeth.

Note: Never let any mango bits get away.

3) The Wedge Way
Also known as The Kayak

CUT off two large portions from each side of the seed as was done in the last method.

Cut each of these mango boats half lengthwise to get wedges.

You now have kayaks.

Save your fingers! Ask an adult for help!

Place one end of the wedge in your mouth and pull out ...

SCRAPING OFF THE MANGO PULP WITH YOUR TEETH.

BITE off the pulp left on the seed.

Stick fingers into mouth to pull out the mango fibres stuck between your teeth.

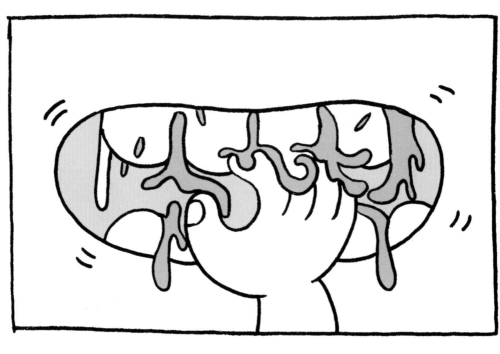

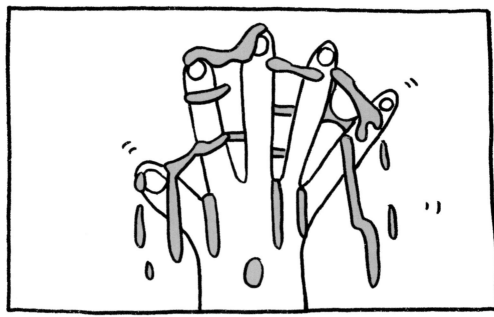

Spend the next hour
TWISTING YOUR FACE IN FUNNY WAYS
as you use your tongue to pry out bits that are still stuck.

Note: The Wedge Way, in the author's view, pulls all the flavours closest to the skin.

4) The Karate Kut Krazies
Also known as the Don't-Try-This At-Home Way

Get the posture right.
Place feet slightly apart,
firmly planted on the ground.

Hold the mango in one hand and keep that arm extended forward.

Keep your other hand close to your body.

Now, throw the mango up in the air.

Wheeee!

As the mango descends, yell

and swish your
hands rapidly in
karate motion
through the
falling mango,
slicing it
mid-air.

KICK A PLATE INTO PLACE

to catch the rapidly falling mango pieces.

Catch the plate before it hits the ground.

Bow, sit back and eat your mango.

Note: This method is way harder than it sounds and needs years of watching martial-art movies before you can master the moves. Not a recommended method.

5) The Everyone-Else-Exit-Now Way

Also known as **The All-Or-Nothing Way**

Also known as **The Mega Mess Method**

Note: Suggested clothing includes chaddi and baniyaan.

Suggested seating is **cross-legged** on a **newspaper-lined** floor, preferably outside your home.

Hold the mango bravely in one hand.

Hand it to an equally brave adult to peel the entire mango with a knife.

Carefully hold the peeled and very slippery mango with both hands to ensure it does not skid across the floor.

Note that everyone else has now fled the room.

Open your mouth, bring the mango up to it and sink your teeth in as deep as they can go.

Rotate the mango and eat till there isn't anything left.

Wipe off the mango pulp and mango juice from your hands, eyes, chin, cheeks and mouth before proceeding.

Clear your nostrils.

Wash your hair.

Wipe the floor.

Wipe the walls.

Don't look up at
the ceiling.
You can't reach it
to wipe it.

Hide your mother's
dupatta that
you used as
a napkin.

6) The Arty Way
Also known as The Turtle

Cut boat-shaped chunks off either side of the seed.

Score the mango flesh (don't cut through the skin) diagonally to make a **criss-cross pattern.**

Push the underside of the mango with your fingers to invert the piece.

 Save your fingers! Ask an adult for help!

There! One turtle ambling along.

A favourite with little kids, this often results in mango-coated yellow noses and mango-smeared yellow chins.

7) The La-Di-Dah Way

Also known as The Oh-So-Proper Way

Cut mango into even-sized cubes.
Place in a bowl.

Pick up a fork. Spear
and transfer the cubes
in the ever-so-perfect
La-Di-Dah Way to
your mouth.

 Save your fingers! Ask an adult for help!

Gently dab the
corners of your
mouth with your
napkin.

Note: Eat it like this if you are in a
restaurant or too lazy to go wash
your hands.

8) The Eat-It-Like-a-Vegetable Way

Also known as Aamras

Cube, blend, flavour with cardamom, saffron or ground ginger.

Eat with a roti or a puffed-up poori.

aamras

Remember to match your personality quiz results to the method of eating!

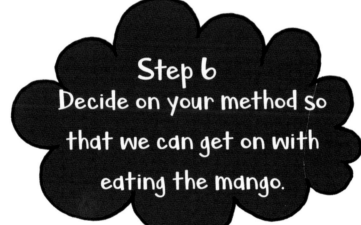

Step 6
Decide on your method so that we can get on with eating the mango.

Decided?

Close your eyes and picture
that mango.

It's the moment you've been waiting for. The moment when you eat your mango.
YUM.

Can't wait! Without further ado ...

On your mark, get set ...

Step 7
... pick up your
mango!

HUh?

WHAT DO YOU MEAN YOU CAN'T FIND IT?

Where did you put it?

How would I know where it is?

Haven't I been speaking to you all along?

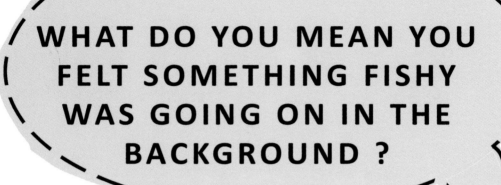

what do you mean I ate it?

Burp. Excuse
me.

KNOW MORE ABOUT MANGOES

A Good Indian Child's Guide

Alphonso

Safeda

Chausa

Sindhoori

Banganapalli

Dussehri

Fazli

Himsagar
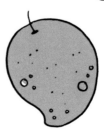

To Knowing Your Mango

Badaami

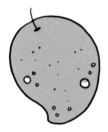

Langda

Tapka

Totapuri

Kesar

Rajapuri

A Good Indian Child's Guide to being a very good Indian child in mango Season

Your friends will have different mango varieties as their favourite. This can often lead to angry words and arguments. Here is how to avoid that.

Be open-minded

Ask for a piece of mango from your friend's plate to compare the flavours again.

Be even more open-minded and ask for even more of their mango, just to be sure.

Be knowledgeable

Get your facts right about why your chosen variety is your favourite.

The best way to research is to eat a lot of mangoes.

Be inquisitive and be a risk-taker

Try mangoes from every corner of India and every part of the world to understand why your choice is the best one.

Be a thinker

Defend your favourite mango till the end of the mango season using all the data gathered through ongoing research.

Be principled

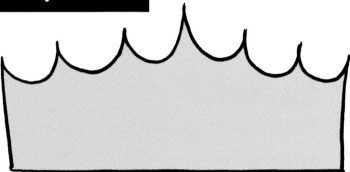

Stick by your favourite mango through every 'Best Mango' argument.

(If you don't have a favourite, now is a good time to pick one.)

The Good Indian Child's Guide to drinking up a mango

Mango Lassi

Ingredients:

2 tablespoons powdered sugar

1/4 cup milk

1 cup yoghurt *

1 cup mango cubes, well chilled

Method:
Put all the ingredients into a blender and whizz away till smooth.

Pour into
glasses and

glug glug glug.

*To make mango milkshake instead, replace the yoghurt with milk. Pour a little milk with the mango and blend before adding all the milk in. You can also add a scoop of ice cream!

Mango Math

Q. If one mango gives you four kayaks, how many kayaks will 18 mangoes give you?

Q. All the kayaks must be shared equally between nine children. How many kayaks will each child get and how many will be left over?

How many seeds
will be on that
plate?

Are you reading this
in mango season?
If you are, don't
waste another
moment ...

Get a
mango
and eat
it!
burp...